PREPARING FOR DISASTER™

ENGINEERING SOLUTIONS FOR WILDFIRES

CAROL HAND

rosen publishing's
rosen central®
New York

Published in 2020 by The Rosen Publishing Group, Inc.
29 East 21st Street, New York, NY 10010

First Edition

Library of Congress Cataloging-in-Publication Data

Names: Hand, Carol, 1945– author.
Title: Engineering solutions for wildfires / Carol Hand.
Description: First edition. | New York: Rosen Publishing, 2020. | Series: Preparing for disaster | Audience: Grades 5 to 8. | Includes bibliographical references and index.
Identifiers: LCCN 2019009929| ISBN 9781725347885 (library bound) | ISBN 9781725347878 (pbk.)
Subjects: LCSH: Wildfires—Prevention and control—Juvenile literature. | Wildfire forecasting—Juvenile literature. | Emergency management—Juvenile literature.
Classification: LCC SD421.23 .H36394 2020 | DDC 363.37/9—dc23
LC record available at https://lccn.loc.gov/2019009929

Manufactured in the United States of America

CONTENTS

Introduction

"It was raining fire," said Roger Gray. Gray was describing the tornado-like "firenado" that occurred during the 2018 Carr Fire outside Redding, California. Alyssa Greenburg and Jason Wilson quoted Gray in their article in the British newspaper the *Guardian*. This fire was so huge and intense that it triggered its own weather system. Towering clouds of fire built up, whirled, exploded, and spread the flames. According to Charles McDermid in the *New York Times*, such firestorms are becoming the "new normal" in California.

The Carr Fire and many others left ruin behind. According to Dale Kasler in the *Sacramento Bee*, 2018 was California's worst fire season on record—even worse than 2017, which also broke records. By November 2018, California had lost 1,627,652 acres (658,687 hectares) to wildfires. The Camp Fire in Butte County became the deadliest fire in the state's history. This fire alone killed eighty-five people, destroyed fourteen thousand homes, and burned 153,336 acres (62,053 ha). It destroyed the entire town of Paradise.

Why is California burning? Michael Wehner is a senior staff scientist at the Lawrence Berkeley National Laboratory. In the *Guardian* article, Wehner blames climate change. California's summers are longer and drier, and winter droughts are more common. Rain is often torrential, resulting in rapid plant growth. Later, when the plants dry out, they make perfect fuel for wildfires.

In an attempt to control the massive Carr Fire, which erupted in California in July 2018, firefighters set and tended to this backfire.

Wildfire destruction is worse than it should be, though. In the 2017 fires, automated calls and digital alerts came too late to help many people. Warnings reached only a small percentage of the population. Keith Schneider, writing for ProPublica, points out that better planning could have prevented the 2018 Carr Fire. Officials could have cleared grass and brush along highways. They could have passed and enforced safety regulations. A better understanding of wildfires is badly needed. STEM concepts—ideas from the fields of science, technology, engineering, and math—can provide a foundation for developing new solutions for dealing with wildfires.

CHAPTER ONE

Brushing Up on Wildfires

Wildfires are uncontrolled and unpredictable blazes. They are strengthened by weather conditions, wind, and an abundance of dry fuel. They burn millions of acres per year, destroying everything in their path. Wildfires occur in many natural environments. They are named according to the type of fuel—for example, forest fires, grass fires, or peat fires. They often begin in wild areas but spread quickly, burning homes, businesses, and agricultural areas.

Wildfire Numbers

More wildfires are occurring in the United States as the climate warms. The two worst years on record as of early 2019 were the years 2017 and 2018. In 2017, there were 64,610 wildfires across the United States; about 9.6 million acres (3.9 million ha) burned. In 2018, there were 55,911 total fires, and 8.6 million acres (3.5 million ha) burned, according to the Insurance Information Institute.

Wildfires occur in every US state, but western states are especially hard-hit. According to the Insurance Information Institute, in 2017, the five states with the highest risk for wildfires were California, Texas, Colorado, Arizona, and Idaho. The ten costliest wildfires have all

The town of Paradise, California, was totally destroyed by the Camp Fire on November 8, 2018; some people relocated, but others in Paradise and Butte County are rebuilding. Many wildfires result in widespread devastation in both populated and unpopulated areas.

been in California—six of them in 2017 and 2018. The Camp Fire ranked number one, and the Carr Fire number eight. US wildfire losses from 2007 to 2017 totaled $5.1 billion.

The United States is not alone. As the climate warms, fire seasons are becoming longer and more intense worldwide. Severe droughts provide an abundance of dry fuel. Logging old-growth forests removes large, fire-tolerant trees. Younger, less-tolerant second-growth forests burn more readily. In 2017 and 2018, Canada (especially British Columbia and Alberta) suffered its worst fire seasons ever. In 2018, a summer heat wave sparked deadly wildfires across Europe. Greece, Spain, Portugal, and Arctic countries including Sweden, Norway,

Finland, and Latvia all experienced deadly fires. In 2015, draining and logging forests led to peat fires in Indonesia.

The Causes of Wildfires

According to Conserve Energy Future, humans cause 90 percent of wildfires in the United States. Only 10 percent start naturally. A few natural fires are caused by erupting volcanoes, but most are caused by dry lightning. This is lightning during storms having little or no rain. Lightning strikes Earth 100 times per second, or 3 billion times per year, according to Steve Nix, writing for ThoughtCo. It is responsible for some of the worst fires in the US Southwest. Most lightning strikes occur in isolated areas in southeastern and southwestern North America. Because isolated fires are harder to reach, they

Lightning is the major natural cause of forest fires. Lightning commonly causes fires during the dry season. Here, lightning starts a forest fire during the wet season.

burn more acres than human-caused fires. Nix also wrote that the average ten-year total of acres burned by lightning-caused wildfires is 2.1 million acres (849,840 ha). Human-caused wildfires burn an average of 1.9 million acres (768,903 ha).

The 90 percent of wildfires caused by humans are almost all accidental. They are caused when people are careless, for example, dropping a burning cigarette butt or leaving a campfire unattended. Burning yard waste, fireworks, auto accidents, and sparks from engines are other typical causes. California's 2018 Carr Fire was started by a vehicle on a highway that suffered a mechanical failure. Some fires are deliberately set. This act is a

Fire Is Natural

Fire, used for light, warmth, and cooking, was one of the earliest human technologies. Even today, everyone enjoys a fireplace or a campfire. Fire is not always destructive. It is life giving, and it shapes ecosystems. In a forest, fire changes the chemical energy of trees into heat energy. It breaks down complex organic chemicals in trees to simpler ones that can be used to grow more trees and other plants. It opens up space to let light in. It changes forest composition. Remaining trees and plants are more fire tolerant. Different combinations of trees take over. Young trees replace old ones. Shrubs and flowers change. In the years after a fire, a burned area may have masses of wildflowers. Natural fires occur in cycles. In drier areas, cycles may be three to ten years long. In moister areas, they occur every ten to one hundred years. When fuel on the ground builds up to a certain level, the next fire occurs. Natural fires produce a dynamic forest. When humans suppress natural fires, though, too much fuel builds up, resulting in uncontrolled wildfires.

crime called arson. Human-caused fires commonly start closer to cities and towns. They often result in the loss of homes and businesses and in deaths.

Sometimes, forest managers start fires to control wildfires. When too much fuel—such as dry vegetation, twigs, and branches—builds up, wildfires may start. Burning off some of the fuel under controlled conditions can prevent wildfires. This course of action is called a prescribed burn. Prescribed burns are not considered wildfires and are not included in wildfire statistics.

A firefighter does a yearly prescribed burn in the Rocky Mountain Arsenal National Wildlife Refuge in Colorado. Prescribed burns are used to reduce fuels to help stop disastrous fires and to create better wildlife habitat.

What Wildfires Are Like

Fires burn when three conditions exist: fuel, heat, and oxygen. These conditions make up the fire triangle. Fuel is any combustible material—that is, anything that will burn. Trees in a forest, dry grass or other vegetation, dead twigs, leaves, and branches are all fuel. Heat starts the fire. Usually, it is a spark from lightning or a human source. Heat also dries out nearby fuel and warms the air. This process keeps the fire going and helps it spread. Oxygen from the atmosphere reacts chemically with the fuel in a process known as oxidation. Oxidation releases heat and produces gases, smoke, embers, and ash.

Three weather conditions make wildfires worse: high temperatures; high, gusty winds; and low humidity. Heat waves and droughts are becoming increasingly common in California and other western states. These weather changes suggest that wildfires will continue to increase in the coming years. Earlier snowmelt and higher average temperatures mean the fire season is lasting longer. However, no single factor by itself causes wildfires. For example, drought will not cause a wildfire unless sparks and high winds are also present.

Daytime fire intensity can be five times higher than its intensity at night. The sun's heat results in higher temperatures, drier conditions, and increased wind speeds. Air currents travel uphill during the day. At night, as the fire becomes less intense, currents travel downhill. Wildfires follow the land up hills and down valleys and are fanned by these wind currents.

Wildfires are unpredictable. They change directions frequently and vary according to weather conditions. There is no way to predict when or where they will start—when someone will drop a cigarette or fail to put out a campfire, for example. This situation makes dealing with wildfires challenging. Engineers are studying various wildfire characteristics. They hope to design solutions that will help predict, follow, and put out future wildfires.

CHAPTER TWO

Cracking the Wildfire Code

According to the Union of Concerned Scientists, wildfires between 1986 and 2003 occurred almost four times as often, lasted almost five times as long, and burned more than six times as much land as fires between 1970 and 1986. In the 2000s, particularly in 2017 and 2018, the number of acres burned shot up.

For the past century, the US Forest Service has suppressed forest fires. This action has caused a buildup of dry fuels on the ground, leading to more fires. Between 1979 and 2015, forest fire areas have become 55 percent drier, according to scientists from Columbia University and the University of Idaho, quoted by Tatiana Schlossberg in the *New York Times*. Fire suppression combined with global warming has lengthened fire seasons from five months in the 1970s to seven months in 2014, according to Erin Biba in *Popular Science*. Some experts say that, in California, the fire season now lasts the entire year.

Where's the Fire?

There are prediction systems for tornadoes and hurricanes, based on weather forecasts. Unfortunately, experts say it is unlikely they can create an accurate early warning system for wildfires. Because so many are caused by

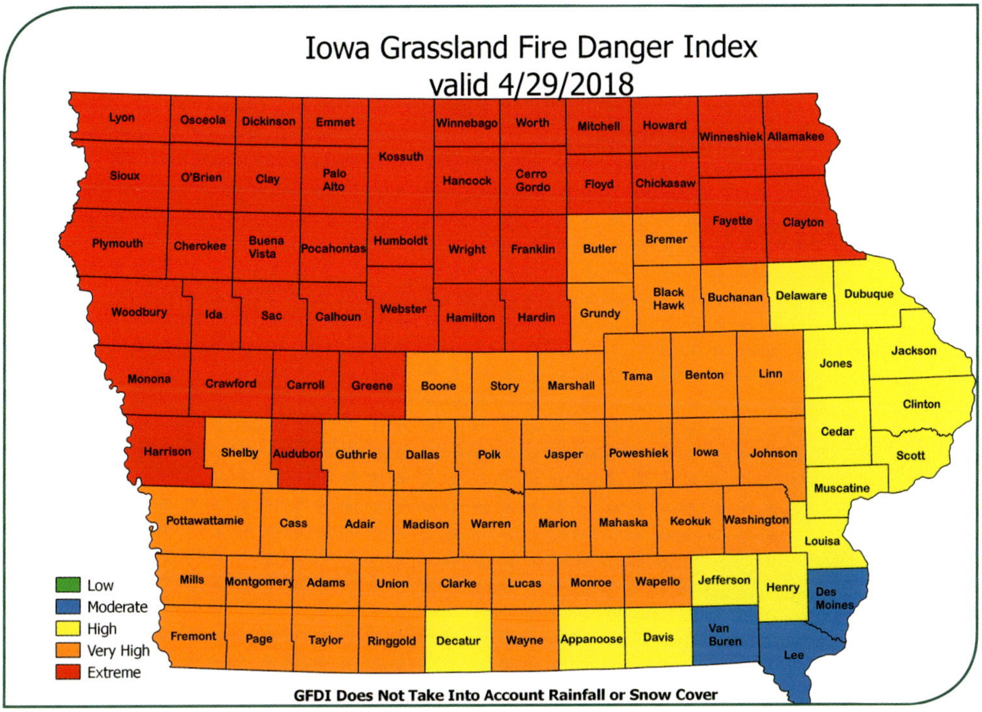

This National Weather Service risk map for grass fires in Iowa shows an extreme risk across the northern counties. It shows a very high risk in the central, east central, and southwestern regions of the state. Charts like this are extremely useful for disaster-prevention experts.

humans, there is no way to know when or where a wildfire will start. Still, fire watchers do issue warnings when conditions are right. Under conditions including drought or dry weather, high winds, and lightning, the National Weather Service (NWS) issues a Red Flag Warning. This notice means wildfires are very likely to occur within the next twenty-four hours.

Wildfires are becoming more dangerous as human populations push outward and cities and suburbs invade fire-prone areas. Fires are more likely to overrun populated areas, destroy property, and endanger lives. According to most experts, the best approach is to educate people to prevent fires from starting. This instruction includes being cautious and prepared in fire-prone areas. For example, people can clear vegetation around their property, prevent sparks by not mowing the grass, not park on dry grass, not drag chains, and not leave campfires unattended.

Modeling Fires

Fire interacts with climate, weather, vegetation, and humans. This circumstance makes fire difficult to predict. State and federal officials

Playing with Fire

One group of engineers makes a living playing with fire. According to a National Geographic video, engineers at the University of California, Riverside, are trying to understand fire by measuring it in the laboratory. Dr. Marco Princevac, at the Department of Mechanical Engineering, and David Weise, a research forester from the Pacific Southwest Research Station of the US Forest Service, study how fires spread. They test a straw-like substance representing dead fuels that catch fire easily and small branches of locally collected green shrubs representing live fuels. They start experimental fires in wind tunnels, which contain instruments to measure the fire's progress. Instruments include cameras and sensors to measure temperature, heat flux, humidity, and the mass of fuel lost. Readouts from the sensors are sent to computers outside the wind tunnel. The engineers try to determine conditions under which a fire that begins in dry fuel will move into live shrubs and how it will spread. In one experiment, they vary wind speed. Higher wind speeds add oxygen to the fire, causing flames to rise higher and fuel to ignite faster. The engineers are building a computer model to predict how fires act under specific conditions.

who manage wildfires are beginning to use computer programs called fire models for prediction. Fire models include mathematical descriptions of factors interacting to cause a fire and keep it burning. They help predict how fires will spread, where officials should send firefighters and equipment, and when citizens should evacuate, or leave the area. Newer, more complex models are more detailed and better able to predict what fires will do. They are based on data from satellites and from recent studies of the nature of fire.

It is difficult to make a realistic computer model. The model is only as good as the information it contains, and model makers do not know all the factors that affect fires or how they interact. Thus, fire models are much simpler than the fires they describe, and their predictions are not always accurate. Fire research concentrates on filling the holes in the knowledge of fire behavior. The new data is used to make the models more accurate.

Scientists and engineers do not yet understand how fires interact with the atmosphere to create their own weather. As reported by Laurel Hamers in Science News for Students, Janice Coen and her fellow scientists at the National Center for Atmospheric Research (NCAR) in Boulder, Colorado, are studying how air moves when heated by fire and how air movement affects fire behavior. They are applying knowledge of weather forecasting to the actions of fire. Coen's group showed how air currents and changes in air pressure helped spread two California fires: the 2014 King Fire and the 2018 Carr Fire.

Modelers are also studying the action of fires at the wildland-urban interface (WUI), where wildlands come in contact with urban or suburban areas. These fires are hard to predict. They have access to a variety of fuels, and they can ignite many buildings, creating a domino effect. Often, they are spread by firebrands, or chunks of burning trees, plants, or debris blown in by winds. Firebrands start new fires wherever they land. A firebrand changes constantly because it burns as it is blown and continually gives off burning embers. Ruddy Mell is a combustion engineer with the US Forest Service. According to

A firefighter from Pigeon Forge, Tennessee, demonstrates the fire department's new interactive Wildland Fire Simulator. Using land contours, it allows firefighters to set conditions and track wildfires.

Hamers's article, Mell and his team are studying how fires burn at a small scale—an area of a few yards square. They develop equations that model how firebrands transfer heat and spread fires.

Fire Models and Satellites

According to Nathanael Massey in *Scientific American*, NCAR scientist Janice Coen found that most fire models are accurate for only about twelve hours. As fire conditions continue to change, the models no longer predict well. The fire travels over varied landscapes, fuel amounts change, and the fire creates its own weather patterns. Coen's group, with scientists at the University of Maryland, is trying to increase model accuracy by adding data to the model from a weather satellite: Suomi NPP. The satellite is controlled by the National Aeronautics and Space Administration (NASA). It circles Earth twice a day, taking photos of a given spot every twelve hours. When new satellite data is fed into the fire model, the model corrects itself, following the fire with much greater accuracy.

A supercomputer called Comet, located at the San Diego Supercomputer Center at UC San Diego, uses a fire behavior model called WIFIRE. According to Lauren Sommer at KQED, WIFIRE combines existing models with real-time fire data from NASA satellites. It runs many simulations at the same time. This operation means it can rapidly forecast what will happen in an ongoing fire. It can help people understand where the fire is going and how fast it will spread. California firefighters field-tested WIFIRE on the 2018 Woolsey Fire in California's Los Angeles and Ventura Counties. WIFIRE is still experimental, and its results varied, but it shows promise for future fire prediction. Still, says Jonathan Cox of the California Department of Forestry and Fire Protection (Cal Fire), fire models are unlikely to replace human judgment because of the dynamic nature of fires.

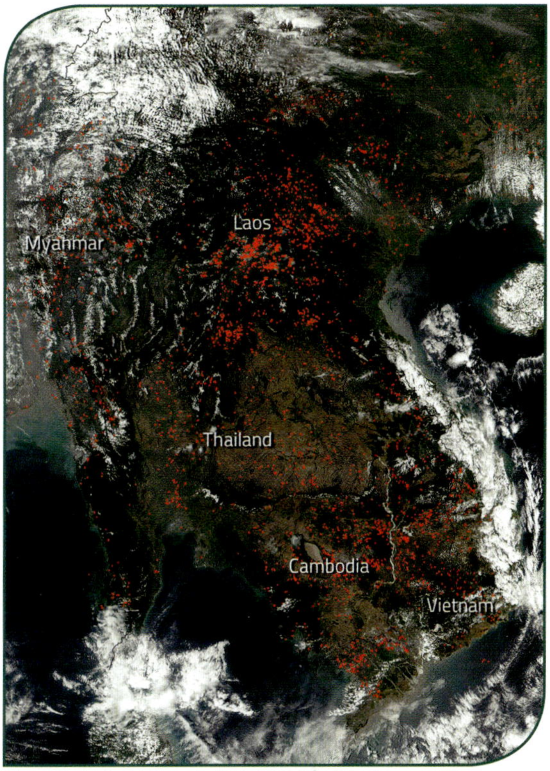

Using special sensors to detect heat on land, the Suomi NPP satellite took this image. It shows more than *two thousand* active forest fires over Indochina on April 9, 2018.

CHAPTER THREE

On the Safe Side of Wildfires

Because people cause nine out of every ten wildfires, simple fire prevention methods can prevent most wildfires before they start. These methods involve common sense and personal responsibility. They can be done by every individual at home and in the wild—no engineers required. Still, scientists and engineers are also getting serious about developing new, more efficient, larger-scale solutions to prevent and prepare for wildfires.

Prevention Is the Best Defense

Individual fire prevention is simple. Around homes and property, people should clean up and remove dead tree limbs, flammable vegetation, firewood, or other potential fuels. They should follow safety rules when burning debris or yard waste. This includes not burning when conditions favor wildfires. People should keep combustible materials, such as oil and gasoline, fuel cans, and barbecue grills, away from areas where fires might start. During dry periods, they should avoid using equipment that might produce sparks, such as lawn mowers or weed eaters.

There are many ways that vehicles can cause sparks, so driving in dry areas is a major cause of wildfires. Exposed wires from steel-belted radial tires can cause sparks when they touch the highway. Dragging chains when towing a boat or trailer causes sparks. Even driving through dry grass can produce sparks. Fire prevention experts urge drivers to carry a shovel and fire extinguisher in their car at all times. They can then extinguish small fires before they become large ones.

This home is protected from wildfires by its surrounding safe zone. This area includes a large defensible space cleared of fuel, and a smaller clean zone, which has only hard surfaces.

No camper should ever leave a fire unattended. Make sure campfires are completely out. This action means dousing the fire with water and stirring until it is cold. According to the Bureau of Land Management, "If your campfire is too hot to touch, it's too hot to leave."

Target shooting is popular on some public lands. In Wyoming, exploding targets used in target practice are a major cause of wildfires. Target shooters should choose a practice area away from flammable materials and should keep a fire extinguisher handy. Of course, everyone should be careful never to drop a lighted match or cigarette, especially in dry areas or regions experiencing high-risk wildfire conditions.

Fire Risk in WUI Communities

Wildfire risks are particularly great in wildland-urban interfaces, or WUIs. The warming climate is increasing wildfire numbers and intensity, and fires are also becoming more dangerous as home building extends farther into wildlands. As wildfires in WUIs increase, firefighters must spend more time and money defending homes.

According to Ray Rasker in *Solutions*, a journal dedicated to a sustainable, ethical future, almost half of the land in the West is public land, such as national forests. The federal government pays for fighting wildfires that start on or near public lands. It also pays

These burned homes in Yarnell, Arizona, were destroyed on July 7, 2013, by the same wildfire that killed nineteen firefighters from the Granite Mountain Hotshots.

to protect homes in WUI areas. Local governments decide how many homes can be built on WUI land but pay little or nothing to protect them from wildfires. The cost of defending homes ranges from about 30 percent of the total firefighting cost to as much as 50 to 95 percent. Sometimes, firefighters die protecting homes. In 2013, nineteen members of the Granite Mountain Hotshots—a group of elite, seasoned firefighters—were trapped and died during a wildfire near Yarnell, Arizona.

Increased home building on WUI lands highlights a need for better planning. Since 1990, according to Rasker, 60 percent of US homes have been built in forested areas, and 40 percent of single-family homes are at risk of forest fires. In the West, 84 percent of forest

Planning for Fire Prevention

Ray Rasker, writing in *Solutions*, has identified nine trends in US wildfires. Four of these trends are things people cannot control:

1. Fires are bigger.
2. Fires burn longer.
3. Fire seasons are longer.
4. The climate is getting warmer.

Because these trends cannot be controlled, they are not helpful in planning for future fires. However, people do have some control over five other trends:

(continued on the next page)

(continued from the previous page)

5. The number of homes built in fire-prone areas.

6. The number of homes that burn.

7. Danger risk.

8. The increase in cost.

9. The increase in firefighting costs as a percentage of county or community budgets.

According to Rasker, trends 5 through 9 should become the basis for future strategies to prevent wildfires. For example, fewer homes could be constructed, and the ones that are built could be built from fire-resistant materials, including concrete, stucco, tile, brick, stone, or steel.

lands available for home building are still undeveloped. This factor means the future wildfire risk in these areas is very great. In 2019, two solutions—fuel reduction and landowner education—were applied to the problem. However, Rasker expects that communities will have to bear more of the cost of protecting homes during future WUI fires. This consequence would require much better planning, including a reduction of the number of homes built in these areas.

Preventing Fires with Science and Engineering

Albert Simeoni, a former firefighter and a professor at Worcester Polytechnic Institute, researches how wildfires can be made less damaging by using simple scientific principles. First, Simeoni says, builders should build houses farther apart. This course of action would decrease the domino effect, in which one burning house spreads the fire to the next house. Also, fire damage can be reduced by preventing vegetation from touching houses, pruning dry leaves, and building with fire-resistant materials.

In 2012, the National Institute of Standards and Technology and the US Forest Service created the first system for judging the risk of wildfires to communities. This system, the Wildland Urban Interface Hazard Scale, provides a scale to show the danger of fire in a given area. It can be used to improve building codes and the standards and practices that would help communities resist the threat of wildfires. It is similar to scales used to assess the damage from earthquakes and tornadoes.

Fire expert Stephen Pyne at Arizona State University says there is no one solution to fire prevention. The solutions may involve technology, cultural change, and politics. According to Pyne, quoted by Tara Lohan in the Revelator in 2018, the wildfire hazard is considered mostly a western event. It is now moving to the East as well, appearing where the houses are. About 79 percent of at-risk communities are located in the South, with recent large fires in Austin, Texas, and Gatlinburg, Tennessee. Pyne sees two parts to wildfire control—fire suppression and prescribed burning. He

When houses are close together, such as these, the risk of nearby houses catching fire is extreme. The Wildland Urban Interface Hazard Scale helps people judge that risk.

Fire Research Group Wants to Douse Wildfire

In 2018, engineers from the Fung Institute of UC Berkeley formed the Fire Research Group to develop solutions for tackling wildfires. They hope to research long-term planning strategies, short-term goals, and real-time solutions for fighting wildfires. Areas of firefighting research include:

- Telecommunications and data collection
- Combustion (understanding and slowing fire)
- Infrared computer vision
- Equipment, both large (transport of water and people) and small (cameras and robots)
- Real-time modeling and prediction
- Health issues related to fires

thinks each area needs to find the right mix to prevent wildfires most efficiently. He says California excels at fire suppression but suffers ever more serious fires. Florida, in contrast, excels at prescribed burning but needs to burn much more. Utah has passed laws making both processes legal. In short, fire prevention is, in many cases, less a matter of science and engineering than a matter of culture and politics. Both processes must be used together to keep people safer from wildfires.

CHAPTER FOUR

High-Tech Ways to Outsmart Wildfire

Wildfire-fighting techniques that are standard procedure in the early twenty-first century will likely continue to be used in the future. They enable firefighters to put out wildfires quickly and safely. A control line is a barrier beyond which the fire cannot (or should not) spread. Some control lines are natural—rivers, for example. Sometimes, firefighters build control lines by cutting vegetation and scraping the area down to bare soil or bulldozing a ditch. Burning out and backburn are techniques used with control lines to further suppress a fire. Burning out involves using torches to burn all brush just inside a control line. Backburn is a controlled blaze set by firefighters just inside the control line. Firefighters direct the backburn fire back toward the wildfire, stopping the wildfire by burning all fuel between the two fires.

In flanking, firefighters attack the fire from the back and gradually work their way around it, spraying as they go. In hot spotting, they assess the hottest parts of the fire to determine the most dangerous areas. When they identify these hot spots, they directly cover them with some combination of dirt, water, and fire retardant. This step is called knocking down. As a wildfire moves, some firefighters carry out cold trailing. They cover

This firefighter has just set a backburn to help control a 2011 fire in Nutriosa, Arizona. A backburn can be an effective way to control rapidly spreading wildfires.

the already burned area, putting out any remaining embers. In an aerial attack, planes and helicopters collect water from nearby sources, such as lakes, and dump it directly on the fire.

Tried-and-True Versus New

Most firefighters want to use equipment and technology that has been tested and proved reliable. Just ask members of Cal Fire, the department responsible for fighting California wildfires. In 2018, Cal Fire announced that, during the next five years, it would buy a

Fighting Fire with … Water Balloons?

William Cleary is a Boeing engineer. In 2007, after his son hit him directly in the head with a water balloon—from three stories up—he wondered, "Why can't we be this accurate with water on fires?" He began experimenting by throwing water balloons off a parking garage and eventually won a grant to study the process. His firefighting concept involves 4-foot (1.2 meter) biodegradable plastic balloons filled with 240 gallons (908 liters) of water and stored in cardboard boxes. The boxes are pushed out of a cargo plane, the wind tears them open, and the balloons explode, spraying water on the fire below. The balloons are dropped high above the flames and aimed with the aid of Global Positioning System (GPS) coordinates and wind-speed calculations. Cleary's plan is now called PCADS, the Precision Container Air Delivery System. A C-130 cargo plane, used by the Air National Guard, can hold sixteen water balloons, or more than 3,800 gallons (14,385 L) of water. A firefighting helicopter can hold more than 2,000 gallons (7,571 L). The balloons can also be filled with fire-retardant chemicals.

dozen Black Hawk helicopters, which were designed in the 1970s. The Black Hawks will replace Huey helicopters, which date back to the Vietnam War in the 1950s and 1960s. Partly, Cal Fire buys old helicopters because they cost less. In addition, Black Hawks have been field-tested in war and proved to be highly dependable.

Another tried-and-true tool is the hand tool known as the Pulaski. This combination fire ax and adze, or hoe, is used to clear brush and other vegetation. Firefighters have used the Pulaski for more than a century. In the late 2010s, the tool was redesigned. It was given a longer handle to help decrease firefighters' fatigue and back problems.

Crews fighting the 2018 Camp Fire in Butte County, California, received help from the California National Guard. A Black Hawk helicopter drops water on the fire.

Although firefighting equipment has changed little in the past forty years, new tools, techniques, and technologies are needed to fight larger, more intense fires. Sometimes, existing technologies are adapted to do more. Helicopters and air tanker planes dump water or fire retardant on fires. Aircraft are also being used for close observation or fire surveillance. Air tankers are equipped with cameras and GPS equipment to follow fires. Information from these tools is fed into computers to improve fire models.

Digital Technologies and Satellites

New types of digital technology may also change the face of twenty-first-century firefighting. An article from *Digital Transformation* lists five digital technologies that could soon transform firefighting: satellites, drones, robots, virtual reality (VR), and the Internet of Things (IoT).

Since 2013, the University of California, Berkeley, working with a Reno company, Fireball, has conducted a project called Fire Urgency Estimator in Geosynchronous Orbit (FUEGO). FUEGO collects infrared (heat) images and other data and develops them into maps. Its satellite and drone technologies monitor early wildfires before they burn out of control. A group of engineers from the University of Alberta in Canada is working on a satellite, called Ex-Alta 2, that is designed to predict, track, and assess wildfires. The satellite is less expensive than others because many of its computer programs are open source, or freely available.

Ground-based robots can fight fires directly. Thermite, a robot developed by Howe and Howe Technologies of Maine, battles wildfires in extreme conditions. It keeps human firefighters safer. Remotely piloted drones, or flying robots, equipped with heat and wind sensors are being used to observe fires from above. No pilots are put at risk, and drones can remain in the air much longer than piloted planes. They can fly at night and into areas that piloted planes cannot. Their information helps firefighters on the ground figure out where to send people and supplies. According to Michael Alba on Engineering.com, a series of drones can

A drone team from the US Forest Service prepares a drone for takeoff. It was used during the 2018 Taylor Creek and Klondike fires in Oregon's Rogue River–Siskiyou National Forest.

be connected by computers. Drone launchpads would be placed about every 10 miles (16 kilometers) around vulnerable communities.

Two other up-and-coming firefighter technologies are VR and the IoT. The US Forest Service uses VR simulators to mimic fire situations and train smoke jumpers, or firefighters who parachute into wildfires. In the simulators, firefighters can change conditions, such as wind speed and direction. This practice prepares them for actual fires and helps them learn to fight fires more safely. Sensors in different areas of a wildfire, such as potential hot spots, can be connected and used to measure temperatures, carbon dioxide levels, and other features of a fire. This example demonstrates the use of IoT technology.

The death of nineteen members of the Granite Mountain Hotshots in 2013 has sped the development of better firefighter protection. The portable fire shelters they used were not strong enough to save them. Josh Fody, a NASA thermal engineer, is developing shelters using heat-shield technology developed for Mars landers. Fifteen of Fody's shelters were tested by firefighters in 2018.

These new technologies may decrease the cost of fighting wildfires. They may give firefighters a head start on fighting fires. Best of all, experts hope they will save lives and protect property.

CHAPTER FIVE

Planning for Future Wildfires

Albert Simeoni, a fire-protection engineer from Worcester Polytechnic Institute, says too little research is being done on the science of fire. People need a much more detailed understanding of how fires start, spread, change direction, and interact with the world around them. Only then will fire experts be able to develop effective ways to fight fires. This understanding is gained using STEM principles, learned in the fields of science, technology, engineering, and mathematics. Anyone who wants to fight wildfires or develop new techniques or technologies for their control must begin with a STEM education.

STEM principles are also important for everyday citizens. As Earth's climate and landscape change, more people risk living in a wildfire zone. Thus, everyone should have a basic understanding of scientific and engineering principles necessary to stay safe from wildfire.

Safety First—Protecting People

The Federal Emergency Management Agency provides guidelines for individuals who need to protect themselves, their homes, and their property from the danger of wildfires. The organization stresses that wildfires can occur any time of year, in any part of the country, so it is essential to be prepared at all times. Cal Fire, California's fire control agency, suggests several ways to make sure people's home and property are protected. It recommends building and maintaining a 100-foot-wide (30.5 m) safety zone around the home. Remove all possible fuels and excess vegetation, and keep the area clean. Construct homes and other buildings with ember-resistant materials. Make a family evacuation kit containing necessary supplies, and keep it updated.

Communication is a vital part of being prepared. Communication requires good sources of information, such as weather reports on local radio and television stations, and text or email alerts sent by communities. For those in danger zones, an NOAA Weather Radio All Hazards receiver is useful. It provides weather and fire notices directly from the NWS. The NWS has three levels of wildfire warnings. A fire weather watch is issued when weather conditions make wildfires likely within the next twelve to seventy-two hours. These conditions include high winds, dry conditions, and high temperatures. A fire weather warning, also called a Red Flag Warning, is issued when fire weather conditions exist and there is danger of fire within the next twenty-four hours. An evacuation notice is issued when a fire is nearby and residents are in danger. It means people should leave the area immediately.

Families need to prepare for wildfire emergencies in several ways. Every family member should know how to use a fire extinguisher and where it is kept. Families should have an evacuation plan. This plan should include several possible routes of escape and ideas for where to relocate if they cannot return after the fire. They should make specific plans for moving small children, people with disabilities, and pets and livestock. The car should be kept filled with gas and have emergency supplies. Every family member should know how to communicate with other loved ones during an emergency. Important phone numbers should be written down and kept in a wallet, just in case one's phone is not usable.

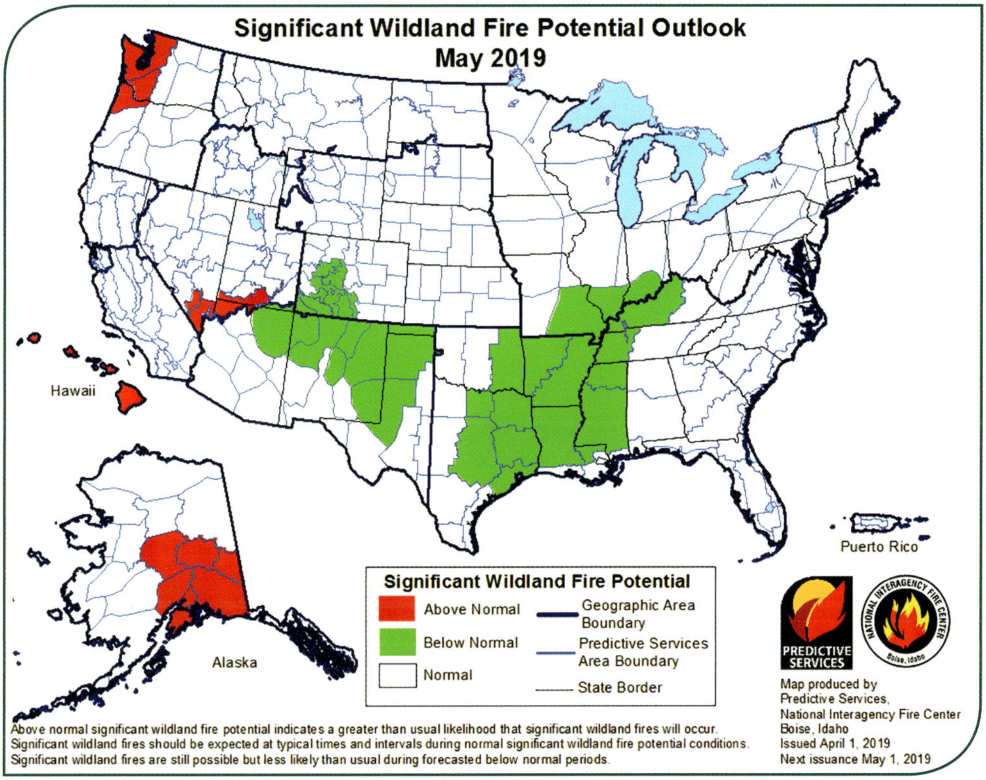

This NWS map shows wildland fire potential for May 2019. Red regions indicate above-normal fire potential. Residents should also monitor NWS radio warnings in real time if there is a realistic threat of a wildfire breaking out or spreading near them.

Safety First—Protecting Communities

Susan Prichard is a fire ecologist at the University of Washington. She studies fire-adapted ecosystems, or ecosystems that thrive when occasional fires sweep through them. Fire-adapted ecosystems show resilience—they recover quickly after fires. In an article in *Fortune* magazine, Prichard suggests that, with climate change and growing

Surviving a Wildfire

If caught in an oncoming wildfire, follow these general rules:

1. Prepare your home before leaving.
2. Evacuate safely.
3. Stay low if caught in the fire.

To prepare your home, first remove combustible material from the yard. Close windows, doors, and vents. Turn off natural gas and other fuel sources. To slow the fire, fill large containers—such as hot tubs, garbage cans, or pools—with water. If the fire is close, officials will order an evacuation. Make an evacuation plan in advance, so you know where to go and what to do. Leave immediately when asked to do so. Wear protective clothing and shoes. If caught in the fire, do not try to outrun it. Look for a water source (such as a pond or river) to get into. If there is no water, find a ditch or low area with little vegetation. Stay low and cover yourself with clothing or soil, damp if possible. Breathe air close to the ground to avoid inhaling smoke. Remain there until the fire passes.

WUI populations, human populations and communities should also become fire adapted. They can begin by reducing fuels and flammable materials around homes, building with fire-resistant materials, and protecting property from burning embers.

The Environmental Health Sciences Center of UC Davis outlines six ways a community can prepare for and respond better to wildfires. First, invest in prevention. This can be as simple as creating fire watch groups for a given area or regularly clearing brush to keep excess fuels to a minimum. Second, develop and test an emergency response system. Emergency alerts should be delivered through all available modern-day channels, including cell phones, landlines, radio, television, and billboards.

Evacuation routes from fire-prone areas should be planned in advance. This planning will decrease injuries and deaths from fast-moving wildfires. Citizens should be educated on evacuation routes and on how to prepare for evacuation. Communities should have emergency shelters set up and fully staffed in advance. Prior planning limits the confusion following a fire.

For the longer term, wildfire experts should work with water and power companies to build systems that will be less likely to go down during a disaster. One major difficulty after any disaster, including wildfire, is the loss of electricity, heat, and water supplies. Lack of these necessities makes life even more difficult for people already coping with loss from fire. Finally, systems are needed to help wildfire victims put their lives back together. They should be able to get food, medical care, and affordable housing. They should also have access to emotional and psychological support.

Wildfires in the Future

Albert Simeoni argues that, to solve wildfire problems, much more research in science and engineering is needed. Otherwise, it will be impossible to protect people and property in WUI areas and in increasingly fire-prone regions around the country. Research should include developing better community design, learning more about how firebrands start fires, and learning how to use fireproof building materials to limit the damage caused by firebrands. Scientists and engineers should also research the interactions of the many factors that cause fires to spread. They should design solutions that can be adjusted to the conditions of individual fires. In a 2017 article

Continued research is needed to find better methods for fighting fires. Here, two researchers from the fire-testing laboratory of Tecnalia Corporation take temperatures during a fire-resistance test.

for the Conversation, Simeoni stresses that this plan requires a tremendous amount of research and a major increase in funding.

Finally, wildfire expert Stephen Pyne would like people to develop a more realistic understanding of the WUI. The WUI is "not really an interface but an intermix," he says in an article in *Pacific Standard*. That is, houses and vegetation are mixed together with no clear-cut boundaries. He points out that, traditionally, people have different attitudes toward fire in urban and rural areas. In urban areas, the attitude is "learn not to burn," while in rural areas, it is "learn to live with fire." The firefighting techniques are very different, and the two groups must learn to work together to solve future firefighting challenges in the WUI.

Glossary

arson A crime in which a person deliberately sets fire to land or property.

combustible Able to catch fire and burn; fuel is combustible.

combustion scientist A scientist who studies fire.

control line In firefighting, a boundary that controls where a fire spreads; it may be natural (such as a river) or human made (a line cleared of vegetation by cutting or bulldozing).

drone A flying robot; it is controlled remotely with a computer flight plan and is equipped with cameras, GPS, and other sensory equipment.

ember A glowing fragment of wood, coal, or other fuel from a dying fire; if moved to a new location, embers can start new fires.

evacuation The orderly removal of all people from an area that is threatened by fire or another emergency.

fire-adapted ecosystem An ecosystem that recovers quickly after a fire, with trees and other plants sprouting from roots or from seeds in the burned soil.

firebrands Pieces of burning trees, plants, or debris blown into an area by winds, which can start new fires wherever they land.

fire model A computer program or model designed to predict how a wildfire will spread; used to decide how to fight fires and protect citizens.

firenado A rapidly rotating, tornado-like column of flames produced by a fire; a weather-like fire pattern that helps spread the fire.

fire-prone Likely to catch fire or be affected by fire.

fire retardant A chemical substance that slows or stops the spread of fire using chemical reactions; often dumped on fires from aircraft.

fire suppression The process of preventing natural fires from starting in natural areas; it allows the buildup of dry fuel and makes wildfires more likely.

fire triangle The three conditions necessary to start a fire: heat, fuel, and oxygen.

flammable Able to catch on fire easily.

infrared energy The type of energy just outside the red end of the visible light spectrum; it cannot be seen but emits heat; a measure of the amount of heat in a body.

internet of things (IoT) The interconnection of everyday objects through the internet; for example, the interconnection of all electronic items in a home.

oxidation The chemical reaction between a fuel and oxygen in the air; it produces heat, gases, smoke, and ash.

prescribed burn A controlled fire set intentionally as a form of forest management. It removes some fuel, making uncontrolled wildfires less likely.

resilience The ability of a system to recover quickly after a disturbance; used to describe fire-adapted ecosystems.

simulation A product of a fire model that imitates, or mimics, the action of the fire.

surveillance The close observation of something, such as a fire, to gain information on its current state and help predict its future behavior.

virtual reality (VR) The simulation or mimicking of a real-life situation or environment with which a person can interact using electronic equipment; VR is used to model wildfires so firefighters can learn to do their job with less danger.

wildland-urban interface (WUI) A zone where wildlands give way to cities, towns, or suburban areas; these areas are at risk for dangerous wildfires.

For More Information

Bureau of Land Management
US Department of the Interior
1849 C Street NW
Washington, DC 20240
(202) 208-3801
Website: https://www.blm.gov
Facebook and Twitter: @BLMNational
This US government agency manages all of the public lands in the country, with goals of conservation, maintaining the health and diversity of fish and wildlife habitat, and sustainably developing energy and natural resources.

Canadian Interagency Forest Fire Center (CIFFC)
1749 Ellice Avenue
Winnipeg, MB R3H 1A6
Canada
(204) 784-2030
Website: http://www.ciffc.ca
Twitter: @CIFFC
The CIFFC provides wildland fire-control services, management, and information to its member agencies in various Canadian provinces. It coordinates with the provinces and territories and shares resources with the United States and other countries.

Canadian Partnership for Wildland Fire Science (Canada Wildfire)
Renewable Resources
751 General Services Building
University of Alberta
Edmonton, AB T6G 2H1

Canada
(780) 248-2033
Website: https://www.canadawildfire.org/about
Instagram: @canadawildfire
Twitter: @CanadaWildfire
This group was formed by several university departments along with the Canadian Forest Service. Its goal is collaboration and exchange of information on research in fire science.

Federal Emergency Management Agency (FEMA)
500 C Street SW
Washington, DC 20472
(202) 646-2500
Website: https://www.fema.gov
Facebook: @FEMA
Twitter: @fema
FEMA is the disaster control agency of the United States. Its function is to help people before, during, and after disasters, including wildfires.

National Aeronautics and Space Administration (NASA)
NASA Headquarters
300 E Street SW, Suite 5R30
Washington, DC 20546
(202) 358-0001
Website: https://www.nasa.gov
Facebook and Twitter: @NASA
NASA is the US government agency associated with spaceflight and space exploration. It is also responsible for the development and launching of satellites, as well as data collection from them, including those designed to study Earth's weather, climate, and wildfires.

National Center for Atmospheric Research (NCAR)
3090 Center Green Drive
PO Box 3000
Boulder, CO 80307-3000
(303) 497-1000
Website: https://ncar.ucar.edu
Facebook: @NCAR.UCAR
Twitter: @NCAR_Science
NCAR is associated with the University of Colorado Boulder. It carries out research on many aspects of the atmosphere, including the interactions of fire and the atmosphere and modeling of fire.

US Forest Service
1400 Independence Avenue SW
Washington, DC 20250-1111
(800) 832-1355
Website: https://www.fs.fed.us
Facebook: @USForestService
Twitter: @forestservice
The US Forest Service is part of the US Department of Agriculture. It is responsible for managing public lands, including national forests and grasslands, and for controlling fire on those lands.

For Further Reading

Black, Vanessa. *Wildfires*. Minneapolis, MN: Jump!, 2017.

Brundle, Joanna. *Heat Waves and Wildfires*. New York, NY: KidHaven Publishing, 2019.

Farndon, John. *Extreme Fires and Floods*. Minneapolis, MN: Hungry Tomato, 2017.

Katirgis, Jane, and Michele Ingber Drohan. *Fearsome Forest Fires*. New York, NY: Enslow Publishing, 2016.

Lewis, Brenda Ralph. *Putting Out Fires: Firefighters*. Broomall, PA: Mason Crest Publishers, 2018.

Palley, Stuart. *Terra Flamma: Wildfires at Night*. Atglen, PA: Schiffer Publishing, 2018.

Perdew, Laura. *The California Drought*. Minneapolis, MN: ABDO Publishing, 2018.

Roker, Al. *Al Roker's Extreme Weather: Tornadoes, Typhoons, and Other Weather Phenomena.* New York, NY: Harper, 2017.

Seigel, Rachel. *California and Other Western Wildfires*. New York, NY: Crabtree Publishing, 2019.

Simon, Seymour. *Wildfires*. New York, NY: HarperCollins Publishers, 2016.

Spilsbury, Louise, and Richard Spilsbury. *Top 10 Worst Wildfires*. New York, NY: Rosen Publishing, 2017.

Thiessen, Mark. *Extreme Wildfire: Smoke Jumpers, High-Tech Gear, Survival Tactics, and the Extraordinary Science of Fire.* Washington, DC: National Geographic Children's Books, 2016.

Bibliography

Alba, Michael. "Using Drones to Fight Wildfires." Engineering.com, December 6, 2016. https://www.engineering.com/DesignerEdge/DesignerEdgeArticles/ArticleID/13841/Using-Drones-to-Fight-Wildfires.aspx.

Biba, Erin. "Predicting Wildfires Could Save Lives. So Why Are We So Bad at It?" *Popular Science*, April 24, 2014. https://www.popsci.com/article/science/predicting-wildfires-could-save-lives-so-why-are-we-so-bad-it.

Conserve Energy Future. "What Are Wildfires?" Retrieved March 29, 2019. https://www.conserve-energy-future.com/causes-effects-and-solutions-of-wildfires.php.

Digital Transformation. "5 Digital Technologies to Help Fight Wildfires." Orange Business Services, August 25, 2017. https://www.orange-business.com/en/magazine/5-digital-technologies-to-help-fight-wildfires.

Dillon, Raquel Maria. "Engineers' Dream to Fight Wildfires with Giant Water Balloons Takes Shape." Boston.com, December 2, 2007. http://archive.boston.com/news/nation/articles/2007/12/02/engineers_dream_to_fight_wildfires_with_giant_water_balloons_takes_shape.

Greenberg, Alissa, and Jason Wilson. "As California Burns, Many Fear the Future of Extreme Fire Has Arrived. *Guardian* (Manchester, UK), July 31, 2018. https://www.theguardian.com/environment/2018/jul/30/california-wildfires-climate-change-new-normal?utm_source=esp&utm_medium=Email&utm_campaign=GU+Today+USA+-+Collections+2017&utm_term=282379&subid=22137556&CMP=GT_US_collection.

Hamers, Laurel. "Wilder Wildfires? Computing Helps Predict Their Path and Fury." Science News for Students, October 1, 2018.

https://www.sciencenewsforstudents.org/article/wilder-wildfires-computing-helps-predict-their-path-and-fury.

Insurance Information Institute. "Facts + Statistics: Wildfires." Retrieved March 29, 2019. https://www.iii.org/fact-statistic/facts-statistics-wildfires.

Kasler, Dale. "Worst Wildfire Year Since When? More California Acres Have Burned in 2018 than in the Past Decade." *Sacramento (CA) Bee*, November 16, 2018. https://www.sacbee.com/latest-news/article221788220.html.

Lohan, Tara. "How Do We Solve Our Wildfire Challenges?" Revelator, October 4, 2018. https://therevelator.org/solve-wildfire-problems.

Massey, Nathanael. "Finally, a Way to Predict a Wildfire's Behavior in Real Time." *Scientific American,* November 15, 2013. https://www.scientificamerican.com/article/finally-a-way-to-predict-a-wildfires-behavior-in-real-time.

McDermid, Charles. "California Today: Experts on Fire Season 2018 Discuss the 'New Normal.'" *New York Times,* May 23, 2018. https://www.nytimes.com/2018/05/23/us/california-today-fire-season-2018.html.

National Geographic. "These Indoor Wildfires Help Engineers Study the Real Thing." June 28, 2016. https://video.nationalgeographic.com/video/news/00000155-978e-df34-ab75-d78ff3750000.

Nix, Steve. "The Origin of Wildfires and How They Are Caused." ThoughtCo, July 19, 2018. https://www.thoughtco.com/the-causal-history-of-forest-fires-1342893.

Pyne, Stephen. "It's Time to Rethink How We Fight Forest Fires." *Pacific Standard*, July 12, 2018. https://psmag.com/environment/only-a-rethink-can-prevent-forest-fires.

Rasker, Ray. "Resolving the Increasing Risk from Wildfires in the American West." *Solutions* 6, no. 2 (March 2015): 55–62. https://www.thesolutionsjournal.com/article/resolving-the

-increasing-risk-from-wildfires-in-the-american-west.

Schlossberg, Tatiana. “Climate Change Blamed for Half of Increased Forest Fire Danger.” *New York Times*, October 10, 2016. https://www.nytimes.com/2016/10/11/science/climate-change-forest-fires.html.

Schneider, Keith. “California Knew the Carr Wildfire Could Happen. It Failed to Prevent It.” ProPublica, December 18, 2018. https://www.propublica.org/article/california-carr-wildfire-failed-to-prevent-it.

Simeoni, Albert. “How to Fight Wildfires with Science.” Conversation, November 3, 2017. https://theconversation.com/how-to-fight-wildfires-with-science-86103.

Sommer, Lauren. “California Firefighters Use Supercomputers to Forecast Wildfires.” KQED, November 19, 2018. https://www.kqed.org/science/1934484/california-firefighters-use-supercomputers-to-forecast-wildfires.

Union of Concerned Scientists. “Is Global Warming Fueling Increased Wildfire Risks?” July 24, 2018. https://www.ucsusa.org/global-warming/science-and-impacts/impacts/global-warming-and-wildfire.html#.XDzckvZFxPY.

Ying, Jessie. “Fire Research Group Launched to Explore Effective Engineering Solutions for Uncontrolled Wildfires.” Fung Institute for Engineering Leadership, UC Berkeley Engineering, November 15, 2018. https://funginstitute.berkeley.edu/news/fire-research-group-launched-to-explore-effective-engineering-solutions-for-uncontrolled-wildfires.

Index

About the Author

Carol Hand is a science writer specializing in earth and life sciences. Hand has a PhD in zoology and previously worked as a college professor and a curriculum specialist. She has written many science and technology books for young people, including titles on glaciers, weather patterns, climate change, and environmental engineering. She also has written books on natural disasters, such as avalanches and tornadoes.

Photo Credits

Cover Ringo Chiu/AFP/Getty Images; cover hexagons (left to right) Nattapong Wongloungud/EyeEm/Getty Images, CHUYN/E+/Getty Images, D-Keine/E+/Getty Images, © iStockphoto.com/Alessandro Rizzo, john finney photography/Moment/Getty Images, Fernando Ojeda/EyeEm/Getty Images; pp. 4-5 (background) Warchi/iStock/Getty Images; p. 5 (inset) Josh Edelson/AFP/Getty Images; p. 7 Justin Sullivan/Getty Images; p. 8 Abstract Aerial Art/Taxi/Getty Images; p. 10 Helen H. Richardson/Denver Post/Getty Images; p. 13 National Weather Service; p. 16 AP Images; p. 17 NASA; p. 19 Joe Amon/Denver Post/Getty Images; p. 20 Laura Segall/Getty Images; p. 23 Mark Ralston/AFP/Getty Images; p. 26 Kevork Djansezian/Getty Images; p. 28 U.S. Air National Guard/Senior Airman Crystal Housman; p. 30 U.S. Forest Service-Pacific Northwest Region/Flickr/File:OAS Drone Team preparing for PSD burn (43615039254).jpg/CC0; p. 33 NIFC; p. 36 age fotostock/Alamy Stock Photo; cover and interior pages graphic elements © iStockphoto.com/koto_feja (spiral design), Ralf Hiemisch/Getty Images (dot pattern).

Design and Layout: Tahara Anderson; Senior Editor: Kathy Kuhtz Campbell; Photo Researcher: Sherri Jackson